Blue Banner Biography

Nancy Pelosi

Amie Jane Leavitt

P.O. Box 196
Hockessin, Delaware 19707
Visit us on the web: www.mitchelllane.com
Comments? email us: mitchelllane@mitchelllane.com

Mitchell Lane PUBLISHERS

Printing   2   3   4   5   6   7   8   9

Blue Banner Biographies

Akon	Alan Jackson	Alicia Keys
Allen Iverson	Ashanti	Ashlee Simpson
Ashton Kutcher	Avril Lavigne	Bernie Mac
Beyoncé	Bow Wow	Britney Spears
Carrie Underwood	Chris Brown	Chris Daughtry
Christina Aguilera	Christopher Paul Curtis	Ciara
Clay Aiken	Condoleezza Rice	Daniel Radcliffe
David Ortiz	Derek Jeter	Eminem
Eve	Fergie (Stacy Ferguson)	50 Cent
Gwen Stefani	Ice Cube	Jamie Foxx
Ja Rule	Jay-Z	Jennifer Lopez
Jessica Simpson	J. K. Rowling	Johnny Depp
JoJo	Justin Berfield	Justin Timberlake
Kate Hudson	Keith Urban	Kelly Clarkson
Kenny Chesney	Lance Armstrong	Lindsay Lohan
Mariah Carey	Mario	Mary J. Blige
Mary-Kate and Ashley Olsen	Michael Jackson	Miguel Tejada
Missy Elliott	**Nancy Pelosi**	Nelly
Orlando Bloom	P. Diddy	Paris Hilton
Peyton Manning	Queen Latifah	Ron Howard
Rudy Giuliani	Sally Field	Selena
Shakira	Shirley Temple	Tim McGraw
Usher	Zac Efron	

Library of Congress Cataloging-in-Publication Data
Leavitt, Amie Jane.
  Nancy Pelosi / by Amie Jane Leavitt.
    p. cm. — (Blue banner biographies)
  Includes bibliographical references and index.
  ISBN 978-1-58415-613-0 (library bound)
  1. Pelosi, Nancy, 1940- —Juvenile literature. 2. Women legislators—United States—Biography—Juvenile literature. 3. Legislators—United States--Biography—Juvenile literature. 4. United States. Congress. House—Speakers—Biography—Juvenile literature. I. Title.
E840.8.P37L43 2007
328.73092—dc22
[B]

                                                                           2007019685

ABOUT THE AUTHOR: Amie Jane Leavitt is a versatile and accomplished author, editor, and photographer. She has written dozens of books for kids, has contributed to online and print media, and has worked as a consultant, writer, and editor for numerous educational publishing and assessment companies. Ms. Leavitt is a former teacher who has taught all subjects and grade levels in both public and private schools. She is an adventurer who loves to travel to new places to gather exciting tales for her writing and photograph beautiful scenery for her ever-growing portfolio. Ms. Leavitt believes that everyone should pursue their dreams, just as Nancy Pelosi has done.

PUBLISHER'S NOTE: The following story has been thoroughly researched, and to the best of our knowledge represents a true story. While every possible effort has been made to ensure accuracy, the publisher will not assume liability for damages caused by inaccuracies in the data, and makes no warranty on the accuracy of the information contained herein. This story has not been authorized or endorsed by Nancy Pelosi.

Blue Banner Biography

Nancy Pelosi becomes the first female Speaker of the House on January 4, 2007. She waves the gavel she will use to keep order in the 433-member U.S. House of Representatives.

Madam Speaker
of the House

Washington, D.C., was a place of excitement on January 4, 2007. Inside the Capitol Building, members of Congress, the media, and spectators crowded the House of Representatives chambers. Everyone wanted to be at this historical event. Today, Nancy Pelosi (peh-LOH-see) would serve her first day as Speaker of the House. She would be the first woman, first Italian-American, and first Californian to ever hold this powerful government position.

Republican minority leader John Boehner (BEH-ner) stood at the podium with Pelosi. He handed her the House's gavel, a symbol that she was now in charge of the meeting. Cheers and applause filled the entire room.

"I accept this gavel in the spirit of partnership," she said as she smiled and waved the gavel in the air. "It is a moment for which we [women] have waited over 200 years. Never losing faith, we waited through the many years of struggle to achieve our rights. We worked to redeem the promise of

America, that all men and women are created equal. For our daughters and our granddaughters, today, we have broken the marble ceiling."

Having a woman as Speaker of the House is a huge milestone. For most of the country's history, women didn't even have the right to vote. Having a woman in such a powerful position in the government is something many people have worked toward for hundreds of years. In the late 1800s, for example, Susan B. Anthony devoted her life to the women's rights movement. Because of the organized protests, speeches, and writings of Anthony and others, not only did women gain the right to vote in 1920, but since then they have been able to rise to important leadership positions. Nancy Pelosi symbolizes the accomplishments of all the women's rights workers who came before her. She hopes to pass this legacy on to other women.

Not only is Nancy Pelosi known as a successful politician, she is also known as a mother and grandmother.

Not only is Nancy Pelosi known as a successful politician, she is also known as a mother and grandmother. Her family came to share this important day with her. After she gave her speech, she invited her grandchildren to join her on the House floor. This made a big impact on all of them. "Because my Mimi got this job, I think more women will get jobs like hers," Pelosi's eight-year-old granddaughter Madeleine said.

Pelosi's grandchildren joined her at the podium as she took leadership of the House floor. The Speaker of the House came to Congress ensure the future for the children.

"I view my role in politics as an extension of my role as mother and grandmother," Pelosi told a reporter. "The reasons I came to Congress are simple: the children, the children, the children. Being a grandmother is a constant reminder of the need to build a stronger future for the generations to come."

> "The reasons I came to Congress are simple: the children, the children, the children."

The festivities continued throughout the day. A concert and a public reception were held in her honor in the nation's capital. Then she traveled to her hometown of Baltimore, Maryland, to celebrate with her family and friends. In a special ceremony, the street where she had lived as a child was renamed Via Nancy D'Alesandro (DAH-luh-SAHN-droh) Pelosi. She said, "I wanted to come back here to say thank you to all of you for the spirit of community that has always strengthened and inspired my life that started here."

Pelosi also visited a statue honoring her father, who used to be mayor of Baltimore. "It is with great emotion that I come to this spot because I used to visit here every time I came to Baltimore," she said.

Pelosi had big goals for her first 100 hours in power. She wanted Congress to pass new laws that would help Americans. She wanted to raise the minimum wage. She wanted to pass laws that would allow scientists to do more stem-cell research. And she wanted the government to reconsider the war in Iraq and bring the troops home.

Nancy Pelosi and President George W. Bush don't always agree on political issues. Even so, the two showed appreciation and respect for each other after the President's State of the Union address on January 23, 2007.

On January 29, 2007, President George W. Bush gave his State of the Union address. He said, "Tonight, I have the high privilege and distinct honor of my own, as the first president to begin the State of the Union message with these words: 'Madame Speaker.' In his day the late congressman Thomas D'Alesandro Jr. from Baltimore, Maryland, saw Presidents Roosevelt and Truman. But nothing could compare with the sight of his daughter, Nancy, presiding tonight as Speaker of the House of Representatives."

Everyone in attendance applauded in agreement. There's no doubt that Nancy Pelosi's father and mother would have been very proud to see their only daughter attain such an important political position. After all, their entire lives had also been dedicated to public service.

Growing Up in Little Italy

March 26, 1940, was an important day for the D'Alesandro family. On this date, their latest addition, a baby girl named Nancy Patricia, was born.

A baby dressed in lacy bonnets, pink bows, and dresses was a new experience for this Italian-American family who lived in Baltimore, Maryland. Thomas J. D'Alesandro Jr. and his wife, Annunciata Lombardi (uh-NUN-see-AH-tuh lum-BAR-dee) D'Alesandro, had five other children, but they were all boys. Thomas III was their first child, followed by Roosie, Hector, Nicholas, and Joseph. A little girl in the D'Alesandro household was a new experience for them all.

Nancy's brothers were immediately protective of her. They felt like it was their job to watch out for their little sister. Nancy enjoyed having five older brothers taking such an interest in her life. She says, "I was pampered in the fact that I had five older brothers, which I highly recommend to anyone."

Six children might sound like a large family to most people, yet Nancy's father came from a much larger clan

Nancy was the only girl in the D'Alesandro clan. For the most part, she enjoyed growing up with five older, and very protective, brothers.

himself. When he was born in 1903, he became one of thirteen children. Because of this, he knew how to successfully raise a large family of his own. The D'Alesandros were organized. They worked together to help each other and serve in the community.

Like most of the residents of Baltimore's Little Italy, the D'Alesandro children were raised with Roman Catholic values. "I was raised . . . in a strict upbringing in a Catholic home where we respected people, were observant, [and where] the fundamental belief was that God gave us all free will and we were accountable for that, each of us. In the family I was raised in, love of country, deep love of the Catholic Church, and a love of family were the values," Nancy says.

Nancy grew up in Baltimore's Little Italy – the same part of town her father, Tom D'Alesandro, Jr., was raised.

The D'Alesandros lived in a three-story row house on the corner of Albemarle and Fawn Streets. They went to the redbrick Roman Catholic church, St. Leo the Great, just a few blocks away. Since Thomas J. D'Alesandro Jr. grew up in this neighborhood, St. Leo's was also where he had attended church and school as a young boy. Nancy's brothers went to school there too.

Nancy was really just an average child growing up. She went to school and took piano lessons. No one would have ever guessed back then that she would someday become a famous politician. "Nancy was a very quiet, shy young lady," says Mary Ann Campanella, one of Nancy's childhood

Tom D'Alesandro was a successful businessman and politician. Here, the family prepares to leave on a cruise from New York Harbor in 1952.

friends. Mary often went to Nancy's house. They would watch television shows together, such as the 1950s children's favorite *Howdy Doody*. As the girls laughed at the silly freckle-faced puppet on the show, Nancy's nanny would make them hot chocolate.

Nancy's family has always been an important part of her life. In particular, she had a strong bond with her father. She respected him and wanted to be like him one day.

Public Service—It's All in the Family

*T*om "the Elder," as Nancy's father was sometimes called, graduated from Calvert Business College. He made a living selling real estate and insurance in Baltimore. Even though the family had much more money than their neighbors, Tom didn't want to leave the blue-collar neighborhood of Little Italy. Instead, he wanted to serve his community by becoming involved in politics.

Tom served in many different ways. He was elected to the Maryland House of Delegates when he was only twenty-three years old. Then he served on the city council for three years. In 1938, he was elected to the U.S. House of Representatives. The race was tight, and Tom won by only 100 votes.

Tom served in the House during Franklin D. Roosevelt's presidency. As a Democrat, he supported Roosevelt's plans to help the nation through the Great Depression. He respected Roosevelt so much that he named his second son Franklin Delano Roosevelt D'Alesandro (he was called Roosie). Tom served in the House of Representatives for five terms.

His next step in politics was as mayor of Baltimore. He was elected on May 16, 1947. Nancy remembers this day well. "Here's a picture when I was a little girl, when I swore my father in when he became mayor of Baltimore," she said in a *CBS News* interview in 2006. Nancy loved being with her father as he performed his public service duties. "We were all in awe of her being the little princess and riding in the open-top cars in the parades," Mary Ann Campanella says of her friend.

Through it all, Tom never forgot the people who had elected him to office. He tried hard to help make the workers' lives easier. One time, a new immigrant in the area, Lou Mazzulli (muh-ZOO-lee), was injured on the job. Tom visited him at the hospital and said, "Recover and I'll help you when you get well." Tom did these kinds of things for a lot of people. Today in the old neighborhood, there are numerous plaques, benches, and parks named after Thomas J. D'Alesandro, Jr.

> "We were all in awe of her being the little princess and riding in the open-top cars in the parades."

Nancy's mother was also involved in public service. She helped with her husband's campaigns and was a leader of the local Democratic Women's Club. Annunciata loved the United States and wanted to be involved in the government. She had been born in Italy and had come to the United States as a young girl. She was attending law school when she married Thomas D'Alesandro. At that time, women did not continue their

Nancy, in the backseat, joins her parents in a political parade in 1948. She loved being part of her father's campaigns.

education and careers after they were married, so she quit law school and started a family. Yet she always stayed active in public service and encouraged her children to do the same.

In 2007, Nancy explained her family's values: "I was raised in a family that was devoutly Catholic, deeply patriotic, and extremely proud of our Italian-American heritage, and in our case, staunchly Democratic. They [our parents] told us that public service was a noble calling. We must work for the public good of all people."

Mayor D'Alesandro's office was on the main floor of the family's home. "We had our doors open every day," Tom III says. Nancy worked in the office and helped the people who would come in needing help with jobs, medical care, and housing. "She got her basic training in politics right in this room," said Nancy's brother Nicholas. "She had an opportunity at an early age to be exposed to the world of politics at the precinct level," Tom III told a reporter in 2006.

As Nancy would travel around Baltimore with her mayor father, sometimes people would ask her what she wanted

John F. Kennedy, left, speaks with Mayor D'Alesandro while Nancy and her mother listen. The meeting with Kennedy was a shining moment in Nancy's teenage years.

to be when she grew up. She once replied, "I want to be a priest so I can help people." Nancy was too young to realize that she couldn't do this. Only men could be priests in the Catholic Church. The next best thing for her to become, she decided, was a politician like her father. That way she could still help people.

This career choice really did make perfect sense for Nancy. After all, she already had a lot of experience. "I've been doing this a long time. I was born and raised in politics, it's almost second nature," she says.

One of the highlights of Nancy's life happened when she was seventeen years old. She had the chance to meet a young senator from Massachusetts at a dinner function she attended with her father. His name was John F. Kennedy. Only a few years later, this famous Democrat would be elected president of the United States. Nancy was also able to attend his presidential inauguration ceremonies.

Nancy's mother wanted to make sure her only daughter received the best education possible. Nancy attended an all-girls Catholic high school in Baltimore called the Institute of Notre Dame. After graduation, she studied political science at Trinity College in nearby Washington, D.C.

As Nancy grew into a young woman, her brothers and father still tried to protect her. Nancy wanted to make her own decisions. "I wanted to be independent. And they were always, you know, 'Oh, you can't do this, you can't do that.' Telling me all the things I couldn't do." They especially wanted to control her dating life. "My parents thought I should stay home with them all the time! If I went on a date, my dad sat in the living room interviewing them. It was really annoying!" she told *People* magazine in 2006.

> "If I went on a date, my dad sat in the living room interviewing them. It was really annoying!"

Yet Nancy seemed to make it through all of these teenage trials okay. While she was in college, she met Paul Francis Pelosi. He was attending Georgetown University, which was also in Washington, D.C. Paul was one of Nancy's first serious boyfriends. They fell in love. After they graduated from college, they were married on September 7, 1963.

Paul was an investment banker, and after graduation he was offered a job in New York City. The two newlyweds packed their bags and moved to the Big Apple.

Mother of Five

*I*t wasn't too long before Nancy became involved in politics in her new home. She went door to door, drumming up support for the Democratic presidential candidate Hubert Humphrey. She also helped out with other causes that were important to her party.

Over the next several years, her work in public service would continue, but it would only be on a volunteer basis. She and Paul had decided to start their own family. In a six-year period of time, Nancy gave birth to five children. Nancy Corinne was born first. She was followed by Christine; Jacqueline; Paul Francis, Jr.; and Alexandra. It was probably difficult to have so many children so quickly, yet Nancy enjoyed her new life as a mother. "When it comes to babies and children, I'm an expert," she says.

Motherhood taught Nancy many important lessons, including the value of organization. "When my children were young, time was my most precious commodity. It made me the ultimate multi-tasker and master of focus, routine, and scheduling."

Nancy was so organized that her kids liked to joke about it. "We couldn't finish one meal without planning the next," Christine once said. Everything in the house ran like clockwork. According to Nancy, it had to be this way.

> "Having five children puts you in a routine," she says. "You find you have to be efficient."

"Having five children puts you in a routine," she says. "You find you have to be efficient. My children trained me to be disciplined and to have a routine, which is very helpful to this day."

While Nancy was busy having children in New York, the rest of her family was staying active in politics in Maryland. Her oldest brother, Tom III, followed in his father's footsteps. He ran for mayor of Baltimore in 1967 and won.

In 1969, the Pelosi clan moved from New York City to San Francisco, California. Paul had grown up in this city and still had family and friends who lived there. It also had outstanding opportunities for his business career. Nancy loved her new West Coast home and was happy to be raising her children there. In fact, it wasn't too long before she started calling San Francisco her adopted hometown.

After the Pelosis moved to California, Nancy once again started helping the Democratic Party when she could. The Pelosi children were raised just like the D'Alesandro children had been. They were shown at a young age the importance

All of the Pelosi children have grown up to lead successful lives. Alexandra, the youngest, is a documentary filmmaker and author. In October 2004, HBO premiered her Diary of a Political Tourist, *which follows the presidential campaigns of 2004.*

of public service. "My children were a tremendous help to me," she says. "As a family, we were all in this together. My children made and served the hors d'oeuvres [for the guests], stuffed envelopes, answered the door and took the phone calls. They were a tremendous help. It would have been impossible to do it without them."

Nancy's parents had wanted her to work hard and get a good education. She wanted the same thing for her five children. As Christine says, "We were always expected to make sure our homework was done; and that we were prepared for what we did. She would always say, 'Proper preparation prevents poor performance.' "

It was this hard work that prepared her children for successful lives. Nancy Corinne graduated from Mount Vernon College and became a hotel executive in San Jose, California. Christine followed in her mother's footsteps

Nancy and Paul Pelosi visit their sixth grandchild in 2006. At the end of the day, Nancy is most proud of her accomplishments as a mother and grandmother.

and pursued a career in politics. She served as the chief of staff for Representative John Tierney from Massachusetts. Jacqueline is an administrator at a children's art school. Paul Jr. is the President of San Francisco's Commission on the Environment. Alexandra became a documentary filmmaker and author.

In 1999, Nancy's first grandchild was born. As of 2007, she had a total of six. "It's great. It's fabulous. It was my goal in life and now I've achieved it. I'm a grandmother," she says.

Family and Politics

*N*ancy Pelosi always felt that she should stay at home and raise her children. Her chance for a career would come later. Once the children were grown, she knew it was time to jump into politics full-time. In 1987, Alexandra was a senior in high school. The other children were in college or married. Nancy knew her moment had come.

In 1987, Pelosi ran in her first political campaign. A seat in the House of Representatives came open when the person holding the position became ill. A special election was held to fill the California 8th District spot. Pelosi ran against other candidates who didn't think she was qualified for the job because of her background. Paul was very successful, and the Pelosi family had millions of dollars. Most of the people who lived in this district had very little money. Nancy felt the money gap didn't matter. In a debate in 1987, she said, "I don't think you have to be sick to be a doctor or poor to understand the problems of the poor. I have spent my life committed to the ideals of the Democratic Party."

The people of San Francisco must have agreed with her, because she won the election. Every two years, she had to run for the office again. Each time she did so, she won. She has held that same seat in Congress now for over twenty years.

> Her views didn't make her very popular with the Republicans in Congress, yet Pelosi's fellow Democrats respected her.

Pelosi has been very popular in the San Francisco area, mainly because she shares the same views as her constituents. She believes in protecting the environment. She wants more work to be done to help people with HIV/AIDS. She feels that all people need to have access to medical care and insurance. She also believes in helping people in other countries. And even though her religion teaches differently, she also believes that women should have the right to choose whether to end an unwanted pregnancy.

Pelosi has worked hard in Congress to get laws on these issues passed. She speaks up for things that are important to her. "When necessary, I'm not afraid to use my mother-of-five voice to ensure I am heard," she says.

Her views didn't make her very popular with the Republicans in Congress, yet Pelosi's fellow Democrats respected her. They felt she was a good leader. In 2001, they elected her minority whip, an important position in Congress. The minority is the party, Republican or Democratic, with fewer members. The other party is called the majority. The minority whip's job is to assist the minority leader on the floor, count votes, and make sure minority

As part of her job as Speaker of the House, Pelosi meets with many important people from around the world. In December 2006, she and Senate Majority Leader-elect Harry Reid met with U2's lead singer Bono, who is also an activist, to discuss the AIDS and malaria crises in Africa.

party members attend important meetings and vote on important legislation. This was the first time that a woman ever held this position. Pelosi did such a good job that in 2002, the Democrats voted for her again. This time it was as the House's minority leader. Once again, this was a first for women.

The highlight of Nancy's career came in 2006. After the November elections, Democrats won more seats in the House than Republicans. Therefore, the Democrats became the majority. Pelosi was selected by her party as the Speaker of the House. This is an extremely important position in the government. The Speaker, who is from the majority, is the main leader of the entire House of Representatives. His or her job is to preside over daily sessions, preserve order in the chamber, appoint committee chairs and members, refer bills to committee, and sign legislation. Besides these tasks, if anything happens to both the President and Vice President of the United States, the Speaker of the House becomes president. Nancy Pelosi became the first woman to ever be so close to the presidency.

Pelosi has a busy life, and she is very famous, yet she tries to keep everything in her life balanced. As Christine puts it, "She understands there's more to life than politics." Nancy has several hobbies. "I do crossword puzzles every day. I just love it," she says. "She really likes game shows like *Jeopardy*," says friend Michael Yaki. "She and I would have these mini-contests … to see who could push the button faster and get the answer."

Pelosi enjoys reading. Some of her favorite books include David McCullough's *John Adams*, *King Leopold's Ghost*, and *Girl with a Pearl Earring*. When people visit her office in Washington, D.C., they notice something else that Nancy likes. She loves to eat chocolate. She has bowls of Ghirardelli (JEE-ruh-DEL-ee) chocolate, which is made in San Francisco, for visitors to sample.

> "To me, the center of my life will always be raising my family. It is the complete joy of my life."

Nancy's favorite way to spend her spare time is with her family. Her husband, children, and grandchildren make up the most important part of her life. Even when Nancy was busy with her 2006 election, she found time to go to the hospital when Alexandra was having her baby. She didn't want to miss such an important day in her daughter's life.

Nancy has worked hard to achieve her political dreams. She advises young people to work hard to accomplish their goals, but to always keep a balance between their careers and personal lives.

Nancy is a devoted mother and grandmother. She hopes her efforts in Congress will help make the world a better place for children everywhere.

Nancy Pelosi gives advice to young people who want a career in politics. "Have a family. Nurture your family, and if you are single, develop friendships and relationships," she says. "Make sure your life in public service is not a total sacrifice of your whole life. Devote time to having a balanced life. Because the success of politics can overwhelm you. You cannot have your personal well-being depend on your political success. This is hard. There will be disappointments and you can't tie everything to it. You must have a sense of self beyond the politics."

Pelosi has become a role model to both women and men throughout the world. Even if people do not agree with her political views, they still respect the way she has lived her life. Not many people can juggle family and career. "To me, the center of my life will always be raising my family. It is the complete joy of my life. To me, working in Congress is a continuation of that," she says.

Nancy Pelosi has worked hard to have both these things in her life. She has shown that many things in life are possible— you just have to be willing to work hard to achieve them.

CHRONOLOGY

1940	Nancy Patricia D'Alesandro is born in Baltimore, Maryland, on March 26.
1947	Her father, Thomas D'Alesandro, Jr., begins his first of three terms as mayor of Baltimore.
1957	Nancy meets U.S. Senator John F. Kennedy while attending a dinner with her father.
1961	She attends John F. Kennedy's inauguration as U.S. President.
1958	She graduates high school, from the Institute of Notre Dame in Baltimore.
1958–1962	She attends Trinity College in Washington, D.C. (now Trinity Washington University); she meets Paul Pelosi while attending college.
1962	She graduates from Trinity College with a bachelor of arts degree in political science.
1963	She marries Paul Francis Pelosi on September 7.
1964	She and Paul move to New York; she begins volunteering for Hubert Humphrey's presidential campaign.
1964–1970	She has five children in six years: Nancy Corinne, Christine, Jacqueline, Paul, and Alexandra.
1967	Her brother, Thomas D'Alesandro III, wins Baltimore's mayoral election and serves for one term.
1969	Nancy moves to San Francisco with her family; she begins volunteering for the Democratic Party.
1976	She manages the presidential primary campaign of California Governor Jerry Brown.
1977–1981	She serves as northern California's Democratic Party's chairwoman.
1981–1983	She serves as California's Democratic Party chairwoman.
1987	She wins a special election as a representative for California's 8th District in San Francisco.
1999	Her first grandchild is born; five more will be born over the next seven years.
2001	She becomes the top-ranking Democrat on the Intelligence Committee; she becomes the first female minority whip in the House of Representatives.
2002–2006	She raises $100 million for the Democratic Party.
2002	She becomes the first female minority leader in the House of Representatives.

CHRONOLOGY

| 2006 | She wins her eleventh term in Congress on November 7. The Democrats take control over the House of Representatives and the Senate. |
| 2007 | She becomes the first female Speaker of the House of Representatives on January 4. |

FURTHER READING

Articles for Young Readers
"Democrats Win Big." *Scholastic News* — Edition 4. November 27, 2006. p. 2
"Pelosi Power." *Scholastic News* — Edition 4. November 12, 2001, p. 2
Rambo, Jeffrey. "A New Congress." *Scholastic News* Online. January 4, 2007.
"Ringing in the New." *Scholastic News* — Edition 5/6. January 8, 2007. p. 2

Works Consulted
Associated Press. "Bush: Pelosi's Dad Would Have Been Proud." *Cincinnati Post*, January 24, 2007. http://news.cincypost.com/apps/pbcs.dll/article?AID=/20070124/NEWS01/701240387/-1/BACK01
Epstein, Edward. "Baltimore's Little Italy to Welcome Favorite Daughter." *Chronicle Washington Bureau*, January 5, 2007.
Fields-Meyer, Thomas, and Jane Sims Podesta. "Lady of the House." *People*, December 18, 2006, pp. 81–82.
Gardner, Marilyn. "Nancy Pelosi, Hero of Grandparent Power." *Christian Science Monitor*, January 17, 2007.
Goodman, Ellen. "Pelosi an Inspiration to Stay-at-Home Moms." *Dallas Morning News*, January 14, 2007.
Gumbel, Andrew. "Nancy Pelosi: Woman about the House." *Independent News and Media*, UK, January 7, 2007.
Hughes, William. "Will Nancy Pelosi Remember Her Populist Roots?" *Baltimore Independent Media Center*, January 6, 2007.
"It Began in Baltimore: The Life and Times of Nancy Pelosi," *SFGate.com*, January 2, 2007. http://sfgate.com/cgi-bin/article.cgi?f=/c/a/2007/01/02/MNG8QNBFNN1.DTL&type=politics
Lewis, Peggy. "Profile: Nancy Pelosi '62. House Democratic Leader." *Trinity Washington University*. http://www.trinitydc.edu/admissions/profile_pelosi.php

FURTHER READING

Marcus, Ruth. "Madam Speaker-Grandma." *Washington Post*, January 16, 2007.

"Milestones: Nancy Pelosi Becomes House Minority Leader." *National Italian American Foundation*, 2003.

"Nancy Pelosi Becomes First Female House Speaker." *Online NewsHour Report Transcript*, January 2, 2007. http://www.pbs.org/newshour/bb/politics/jan-june07/pelosi_01-02.html

"Nancy Pelosi: Two Heartbeats Away." *CBS News*, October 22, 2006. http://www.cbsnews.com/stories/2006/10/20/60minutes/main2111089.shtml

"Pelosi: 'Let Us Work Together.'" *CNN.com* transcripts, January 4, 2007. http://www.cnn.com/2007/POLITICS/01/04/pelosi.transcript/index.html

Povich, Elaine S. "Her House." *AARP Bulletin*, January 2007. pp. 30–31.

Salmon, Stephanie. "10 Things You Didn't Know about Nancy Pelosi." *U.S. News & World Report*, November 7, 2006. http://www.usnews.

Schroeder, Pat. "Pat Schroeder on Nancy Pelosi." *Ms.*, January 16, 2007. http://www.msmagazine.com/radar/2007-01-16-friedman.asp

Smith, Patricia. "Breaking the Marble Ceiling." *The New York Times Upfront*, January 2007. http://teacher.scholastic.com/scholasticnews/indepth/upfront/features/index.asp?article=f1211b

Symington, Gaye. "The View from the 'Ladies' Gallery' as Pelosi Is Named House Speaker." *Burlington Free Press*, January 16, 2007. http://www.burlingtonfreepress.com/apps/pbcs.dll/article?AID=/20070116/OPINION/701160321

"Thomas D'Alesandro Jr. — Biographical Information." *Biographical Directory of the United States Congress.* http://bioguide.congress.gov/scripts/biodisplay.pl?index=D000007

Walsh, Deirdre. "Pelosi Becomes First Woman Speaker." *CNN.com*, January 5, 2007. http://www.cnn.com/2007/POLITICS/01/04/congress.rdp/index.html

Wyatt, Kristen. "Pelosi Visits Hometown on Victory Tour." Associated Press. *CBS News*, January 5, 2007. http://www.cbsnews.com/stories/2007/01/05/ap/politics/mainD8MFCOBG2.shtml

Wyatt, Kristen. "Speaker-to-be Pelosi Learned Politics in Baltimore Row Home." Associated Press. *Sign On San Diego*, December 26, 2006. http://crossword.uniontrib.com/news/politics/20061226-1337-pelosisbaltimore.html

On the Internet:

Congresswoman Nancy Pelosi, California, 8th District:
    http://www.house.gov/pelosi/

Office of the Clerk, U.S. House of Representatives, "Kids in the House."
    http://clerkkids.house.gov